"Pieces of Me: Poetry and Prose"

By

Tanni Haas

Contents

Part I:

Poems (Recollections)

Greetings

Beneath every greeting
A lifetime more
And always already
An ever-shifting, constant floor
Of questions that could have been asked
And a single, imperfect place to hide

The Mirror

The mirror shows a shadow
Only I recognize
I can reach for it
Or walk away
Or I can step aside
And let it fall where it may

I

I try to walk a straight path
With closed eyes and clenched fists
On a rounded earth
The wind could be much stronger
Tomorrow could be much better
I could be someone else

A Puzzle

A puzzle lies before me
Or so they say
When I reluctantly lower my head
And submit
Why can't it be as simple
As one step before the next?

My Parents

Early summer: My parents are visiting from abroad
They are standing in my living room
As far apart as the space allows

I watch with curiosity as
They launch themselves
In the weak morning light

It's been a long time, so long
That I no longer remember
What my blood tastes like

Pieces

If you decide to pick up the pieces
Don't pick them up
One at a time
Or you will cut yourself
Even more

Forgiveness

I see you
As you once were
Not caught in a long-forgotten pose
Or fleeing to a vanishing point in the distance
But calmly and free of any guilt

Just Like Us

We stand by the water's edge
Wondering what might happen next
And far beyond a faint, curved line
Another life perhaps
And even further another couple
Just like us

Life

It used to be so simple
Not life, life is never simple
But that other thing
We call love
The way our hands moved
Our breaths
How we breathed
Life

Our Dance

We dance our dance
As though the dance matters
One step here, one step there
As though our feet will always find a way
Back to where we were
As though the ground beneath our feet
Will always be there when we need it
As though it is the dance that matters
And not the dancers

Part II:

Microfiction (Pieces of Me)

The Void

It was only after he got back on the bus that would take him the long road home that he began to realize what he'd accomplished.

It had started that morning with an unexpected phone call from an ex-girlfriend whom he hadn't seen or heard from in almost two decades. After some polite small talk, she revealed why she was calling. She'd decided to let him in on a secret that she'd kept from him all these years: he was the father of a boy that she'd given birth to after their relationship had ended.

The news hit him like nothing before, and it wasn't that he never knew she was pregnant in the first place. Rather, he'd always felt a profound void in the center of his being, and now he finally understood what that void was all about: he was a father who'd missed out on being a father. Where there was emptiness there should have been an abundance of memories, and emotions, and excitement about the future. He was so exhilarated that he could barely contain himself when she offered that he could come and visit them later that evening.

She opened the front door so quickly after he rang the bell that it seemed as though she, too, had been anticipating this moment all day. The house was dark but he could see the shadow of a tall, slender person towering right behind her. Instead of greeting them and stepping into the hallway, he just stood there and stared. The young man so clearly wasn't his son, and he knew that his ex-girlfriend knew that. Both of them were unusually short and stout.

As he sat down in the back of the bus with a full view of the landscape on both sides of the road, he took in a deep breath of relief. He wasn't the boy's father so he could now eliminate missing out on fatherhood from the list of possible sources of his discontent. He'd gotten one small step closer to discovering the true source of the void that he was feeling. Not bad for a day's work.

The Affair

He arrived at the agreed-upon street corner 15 minutes early. It was awkward to try to stay in place with the constant stream of passersby from both directions but he didn't want to run the risk of getting there later than her. Also, she'd insisted that they meet in a busy, public place.

He'd always been attracted to her but hadn't acted on it for good reasons. He sensed that his feelings were reciprocated but wasn't entirely sure. When he finally decided to make his move at a large family gathering she reacted very strongly, saying that she couldn't do that to her own sister, that it was morally wrong and would make her feel incredibly guilty. But the way she responded made him think that she was secretly intrigued by his proposition.

He kept calling her over the next couple of weeks and, when she finally relented, she suddenly seemed eager to have a say in the practical arrangements. She decided when and where to meet, at what time, and most titillating of all asked him to pay for a room at a nearby hotel.

All the color drained from his face when he saw who turned the corner and headed towards him with rapid strides. There came his wife in all her glory. That was the only part of the plan that they, or rather he, hadn't properly prepared for.

The Thief

He could both hear and see what was going on from his hiding place under the bed. He could hear their voices on the other side of the door and, when he shone his flashlight under the door frame, he could see the shadows of their feet moving through the light. He was lying as still as he could, although his position offered no actual protection if they were to come for him.

He shouldn't have taken all of it. It had started with a few coins here and there. He'd meant to put them back but he didn't. After the first couple of times, he'd found a note with the money. The note said that they knew what he was doing and that he better stop before it was too late. He'd never felt so visible in his life. All his senses were heightened. Now it really was too late.

He wondered when they'd come for him and feared what they'd do when they did. He could hear their voices getting louder and more animated and then saw two feet moving rapidly towards the room. Without even knocking on the door, his father swung it open and shouted: "Get back to bed and go to sleep. I'll deal with you tomorrow!"

The Pain

He doesn't know what to do. The pain is almost unbearable. He misses her so much.

He tried to write a letter to her. But the right words didn't come to him, the words that would bury themselves deep into her heart and stay here. Now he's pacing around the living room in endless circles. Once in a while he walks over to the window and stares into the darkness even though he knows he won't find her there.

If he turned around and walked into the bedroom, he'd find her in a chair next to the packed bags. But that wouldn't make a difference. She knows what to do.

How Do You Say Goodbye (If You Never Said Hello)?

The scene is a familiar one: a hospital room, a bed with a father who's dying of a serious illness, and a son who's sitting in a chair next to the bed.

The son is uncertain about what he should do. Should he go look for a vase for the flowers that he's brought for the father? Should he say something first? What should he say?

The father was asleep when the son entered the room. The son sat down in the chair with the flowers in his hands to avoid waking up the father. It's too late now. The father has woken up. What should he say?

Luckily, the son doesn't have to say anything. A nurse enters the room to check the father's vitals. It's doesn't look good.

The son gives the flowers to the nurse. She promises to look for a vase for the flowers and bring it back to the father.

The son's anxious and wants to leave, but how do you say goodbye if you never said hello?

The Girl Who Threatened To Swallow Me Whole

When I was six or seven, I no longer remember my exact age, an older girl at my school whom I'd never seen before approached me one day on the playground during recess. Without any warning or explanation, and without any signs of emotion, she told me that she'd swallow me whole if she ever encountered me again. I got so frightened that for many months afterwards I roamed the hallways every day on the lookout for an empty space where I could hide from the girl and any curious teachers until recess was over and I safely could get back to my classroom.

One day, as I sat in the back of one of the supply closets reading a large picture book, I heard a sudden noise, cautiously lowered my book, only to find that my tormenter was standing right in front of me. I'd no idea how she'd found me or how long she'd been there.

I sat there, paralyzed with fear, thinking that I only had a few moments left to live. She opened her mouth widely and demanded that I stand up and put my face right next to it. As I moved closer, I could feel, first, her warm breath, and then her jagged teeth against my skin.

In that moment, I realized, I was far too big for her to swallow whole. I opened my mouth a wide as hers and stared back at her. After a few minutes of glaring into each other's mouths, she gave up and walked out, leaving me standing triumphant in the supply closet.

I wasn't frightened after that and I no longer needed to search for an empty space at recess. Although, sometimes I still did, just so I could read my picture book in peace.

Opportunities

When he turns the corner, he stops. What has happened to his street? Where's everything he's familiar with? Instead of buildings and people and animated conversations, there's nothing but grass everywhere and a mountain range in the distance.

He stands at the edge of the grass and looks around at the transformed landscape. What is he to do? How is he supposed to get home? But the longer he thinks about it, the less hopeless the situation begins to appear. Why not take advantage of the new circumstances.

He spreads out his jacket on the grass, lies down on it, and starts to make plans for the future. Yes, tomorrow he'll walk to the mountains, search for the tallest one, climb to the top, and build a new home there for himself. He feels young, energetic, and ready for whatever lies ahead.

The Garden

It had started innocently enough. One morning, as he sat on the terrace admiring his carefully-manicured garden, he noticed that something was amiss: a part of the garden wasn't entirely plane.

He went to the shed, picked out a shovel, and started to dig into the offending part. But every time he stepped back to assess whether he'd achieved his goal, he noticed that a new part of the garden stood out from the rest. Out went the tulips, the rose bushes, and all the other colorful flowers.

In the end, only the cold, soft soil was left. Exhausted, he lay down on his back, closed his eyes, and let the soil calm his body. It felt like the end to something, or perhaps the beginning of something new. He wasn't sure.

My Colleagues and I

We're in the middle of a discussion, my colleagues and I, that concerns our very future together. One raises his voice in anger, another meekly retreats, a third tries her best to mediate. And back and forth the words ricochet across the conference table.

If a giant hand were to come down from above and replace us with another set of colleagues, the discussion would continue uninterrupted.

The Conversation

They began to talk as soon as she sat down next to him. It was the middle of the night, the bus was driving fast but soundlessly down the highway, and he could hear every word she said as clearly as if they were the only two people left in the world.

He must have dozed for a while. When he opened his eyes, the seat next to him was empty.

Looking back, he liked to think of it as one of the most intense conversations he could have had.

Part III:

Microfiction (Fathers and Sons I)

Sleepless

He finds himself retreating to the bedroom several hours before he starts to get tired. The narrow space, with its black-out curtains and heavy comforter, helps slow down his racing mind. Or at least somewhat.

He can't stop thinking about whether his son is asleep. He's still a toddler so he should be sleeping peacefully and without a care in the world. But he used to wake up in the middle of the night and just lie there and stare frightened into the darkness with his pacifier nowhere to be found. It can be lonely at night and very scary, with monsters lurking in every shadow.

He'd go and check up on him if he could but he can't. Since the divorce, he's only seen him for a couple of hours every other weekend. Hopefully, one day.

Like Father, Like Son?

As he's driving up the country road to his son's first sleep-away camp, he can't help but think back on his own experiences, on how weak and fearful he felt in the presence of all those self-confident campers, on how he spent most of his energy trying to make himself as invisible as possible, wishing only for camp to be over so that he could get back to the safety of his usual, solitary existence.

It's summer and the sun is shining down from a clear sky on a world full of new beginnings. When they arrive at the camp, he cautiously unlocks the backdoor so that his son can jump out and into the light.

The Moment

The moment he realizes he doesn't know where his son is is the moment he ceases to exist as a person and becomes reduced to two eyes and a body that frantically search the crowds of toddlers at the local playground. Even when his son eventually pokes his head out from behind a tree as though they've been playing a game of hide-and-seek the whole time does he not fully regain himself. It feels as though he'll always be a little different, a little less, than he used to be.

Letting Go

He's running next to the bicycle with one hand on the handlebars. The moment he tries to let go, he can't.

As his son takes off, his only thought is when will he turn his head and look back.

Memories

When his son isn't home, he likes to go into his bedroom, lie down on his bed, and let his eyes rest on all the things he's accumulated over the years. His son's absence makes it easier to bring the past into the present.

One day, when the best he can hope for is a visit now and then, he'll lock the door to the bedroom and hide the key from himself.

After The Funeral

After the funeral, they walk back into the house. His arm is around his son's slender shoulders.

His son still has a lot to share. The words are coming out in no particular order.

Out in the garden, under a foot of soil, lies their loyal companion. The loss is much deeper.

Vacation

He feels the pressure long before they arrive at their destination. His head is hurting from trying to come up with activities that'll leave a lasting memory of their time together.

In the evening, when they get back to the hotel room, his son asks if he can lie next to him on the bed and watch television.

Growing Up

As he browses through a magazine, he looks over at his son who's engrossed in a book.

In a moment, he'll get up from the couch, walk over to the recycling bin, toss the magazine in it, and never think about it again.

What happens to us when we grow up?

Waiting To Exhale

His son is lying in the hospital bed looking quietly out the window on the falling snow. From his nose and mouth run tubes to equipment that's attached to the side of the bed.

Once in a while, the equipment makes a loud sound and a team of doctors and nurses comes rushing into the room. He can barely see his son from behind their crouching backs.

He holds his breath and waits. He helped give life to his son but he can't make him breathe.

How Little Did He Know

It's hard to forget the day his son looked up at him with his big, blue eyes and asked if he knew everything.

How little did he know.

Part IV:

Microfictions (Fathers and Sons II)

The Photograph

The photograph shows his elderly father holding his infant grandson tenderly against his chest, with the grandson's tiny face just visible over his shoulder. The infant's eyes are glossy, like he just woke up from a nap.

His elderly father is looking straight at the camera. He knows exactly what he wants him to think: if only the circumstances had been different, I could have protected you, too.

Shame

His father used to chase him around the house when he got home from work in the evening. Eventually he'd catch him, and he'd beat him. He'd beat him until he'd no choice but to cover up the bruises with extra clothing and a pair of sun glasses in school the next day.

Shame isn't going to claim his own son. He'll make sure of that.

Personality Changes

People often change when they learn they have a terminal illness. Some become softer, more amenable to others. Others resign themselves to their fate and wither.

Not his father.

Stirring The Soup

The house is quiet when he returns home the next morning. He's no choice but to go into the kitchen where his father is stirring a big pot of soup. His father doesn't look up from the pot when he tries to explain himself, but his disapproval couldn't be clearer from how the ladle cuts through the broth like a knife.

Weekends

On weekends, his father always retreated to his bedroom right after lunch.

He'd lie there, like a hibernating bear, with his face turned to the wall. Unlike a bear, he'd only rise when the house was as dark as the evening outside.

The Umbrella

They say that there's nothing worse to a child than unpredictability.

He's not so sure about that. His father was nothing if not predictable. He always towered over him like an umbrella that, instead of keeping him safe from the rain, made it impossible to see the sun.

The Real Family

He only ever saw his father happy in the company of his two brothers - his real family.

When they came to visit, they'd sit right next to each other in the couch and talk and laugh.

He felt like he was watching a diorama from another time and place. He could see and hear them, but he meant nothing to them.

The Garden

In the summer, when he played by himself in the garden until late in the evening, his father would often sit on a chair by the window.

He felt his eyes follow him around the garden as he played, but he could have been mistaken. It could just as well have been his own reflection in the darkening window pane.

Touch

The first time he touched his father was also the last time.

His asked him to help adjust his disappearing body, but he could barely get himself to touch the arms. He let them slide through his hands as though he didn't have the strength to hold them back.

Swimming Lessons

Unlike the other children, he couldn't learn how to swim no matter how hard he tried.

When his father picked him up after his lessons, he told him elaborate stories about all the praise the instructor was lavishing on him.

They never did go into any body of water together.

Part V:

Dialogues (Relationship Pieces)

(1)
She: Are you in?
He: You know that I am
She: I don't
He: Trust me
She: Why?
He: Because I'm here
She: What about tomorrow?
He: I don't know
She: I do
He: I'm not you

(2)
He: Let's go
She: Go where?
He: Out
She: Out where?
He: It doesn't matter
She: Why go?
He: There'll be people
She: And?
He: It'll be fun
She: How?

(3)
She: I want it
He: But it'll never be the same again
She: It'll be even better
He: How can you be sure?
She: I can feel it
He: I can't
She: It's important to me
He: What about me?
She: You're also important to me
He: I hope so

(4)

He: Be careful
She: He needs to learn
He: But he's so young
She: Not too young
He: He needs our help
She: You're not helping him
He: Of course I am
She: You're doing it for him
He: I want the best for him
She: Exactly

(5)
She: How could you?
He: I don't know
She: That's not good enough
He: I know
She: What do you know?
He: That it was wrong
She: So why did you?
He: I couldn't help it
She: I can't help you
He: How could you?

(6)
He: What's up?
She: I'm ready
He: Ready for what?
She: Something new
He: Anything new?
She: Anything new
He: It sounds scary
She: It could be
He: Can I come?
She: We'll see

(7)
She: What do you think?
He: It's a great idea
She: What's a great idea?
He: What you suggested
She: I didn't suggest anything
He: What do you mean?
She: I asked your opinion
He: Why did you do that?
She: You're not listening to me
He: You're not listening to me

(8)
He: Why are you so angry?
She: Because I'm right
He: Isn't that strange?
She: What's strange?
He: That you're always right
She: That's not true
He: Do you see the irony?
She: What irony?
He: In what you just said
She: No

(9)
She: What a lovely place you picked
He: Thanks
She: I'm so happy to be here with you
He: Me too
She: It's been a while
He: It has
She: Much too long
He: I agree
She: What do you want to do later?
He: That's up to you

(10)

He: Why didn't you tell me this before?

She: I didn't think it mattered

He: You didn't think it mattered?

She: No

He: It changes everything

She: You can't be serious

He: I feel like I don't know you

She: I am who I've always been

He: I'm beginning to see that

She: I don't like where this is going

(11)
She: So?
He: So what?
She: You shouldn't be asking
He: Why not?
She: Asking kills it
He: You're exaggerating
She: I don't think so
He: I think so
She: You just killed it
He: How?

(12)
He: I think you've had enough
She: Why would you say that?
He: Because it's true
She: I'd never say that to you
He: That's true
She: Do you know what's even worse?
He: No
She: That you'd say that in public
He: What do you mean?
She: Look around you

(13)
He: I heard you coughing
She: Yes, I was coughing
He: Were you up all night?
She: I was
He: I'm sorry
She: I'm sure you are
He: I must have fallen asleep
She: You were tired
He: How are you feeling now?
She: I just took some medication

(14)
He: What do you think?
She: It looks great
He: You don't sound excited
She: I am
He: Should I do more?
She: You could
He: So you don't like it?
She: I do
He: I give up
She: Why?

(15)
She: When are you going to be back?
He: I don't know
She: But you must have an idea
He: I don't
She: How is that possible?
He: Why do you keep asking?
She: I just want to know
He: But I don't know
She: I'll be fine
He: So will I

(16)
She: I can't feel anything
He: I know
She: It hurts too much
He: I know
She: What should I do?
He: You're doing it
She: I am?
He: You are
She: I need your help
He: You're getting it

(17)
He: I totally forgot
She: How could you?
He: I'm so sorry
She: You should be
He: I'll make it up to you
She: Make it up to me?
He: Yes
She: How are you going to do that?
He: You'll see
She: Don't forget

(18)
She: You should go on
He: What about you?
She: I can't make it
He: I'll help you
She: You don't have to
He: But I want to
She: That's nice of you
He: I'm nice
She: You're too nice
He: Perhaps

(19)
He: It'll be over soon
She: Don't say that
He: But it's true
She: It doesn't matter
He: I think it does
She: I don't want to talk about it
He: Talking helps
She: Not me
He: It's not about you
She: But it will be

(20)
She: Are you there?
He: I'm here
She: I can't see you
He: I know
She: I can't feel you
He: I know
She: I miss you
He: I know
She: I can't hear you
He: I can't hear you